The
HERO
EFFECT

Being Your *Best* When it Matters the *Most!*

KEVIN BROWN

The **HERO** Effect

Being Your *Best*
When It Matters the *Most*

First edition published August 2017 by Kevin Brown Enterprises, LLC/
  Apple Pancakes Publishing

Printed in the United States of America

ISBN: 978-0-9600155-0-4

Credits:

Copy editor	Kathleen Green, Positively Proofed, Plano, TX, info@positivelyproofed.com
Additional editorial services	Ellie Maas Davis
Design, art direction, and production	Melissa Farr, Back Porch Creative, Frisco, TX, info@BackPorchCreative.com
Original cover design	Kayleigh Lohse, LolaGrey Creative, Portage, MI, kayleigh@lolagreycreative.com

Foreword

Seldom in my life have I been as inspired and moved by a book as I have with the book that you are holding in your hand.

I am willing to bet that you will say the same after you read it.

Sprouting from a sheet of yellow notepad paper with one handwritten word on it—HERO—is the true-life story of my friend Kevin Brown. This year, Kevin will share his story and inspire thousands of people across the world. It will inspire you, too.

Why is Kevin's story so engaging to everyone who reads his words or listens to him speak? I think it is because Kevin is one of us ... a typical person who has prospered through some very tough times. His message is one that each of us can relate to.

The Hero Effect begins with a story of Lisa, a calm, positive, loving wife who provided Kevin the insight to recognize who heroes really are. Lisa encouraged him to look beyond the image reflected in his mirror and pay attention to the images of the people surrounding Kevin who, in fact, were his heroes. Her simple advice was for Kevin to share his heroes' stories.

This book is also about apple pancakes. That may not sound like something to write a book about, but don't make that judgment until you read the story. *The Hero Effect* introduces us to an incredible young man and his relationship with his parents and a chef named Bea. You will discover how one person positively influenced the life of a family … while at the same time was the recipient of increased knowledge and awareness that changed a huge, successful organization.

Kevin Brown is one of my heroes. The HERO acronym that Kevin introduces us to in this book describes why he is my hero.

Kevin is one of the most **h**elpful people I have ever met. He is interested in making all of our lives better and, with his words and wisdom, has provided us inspiration to become our very best.

Kevin is **e**xceptional. He is a master storyteller and one of the best speakers on the planet. His message is sincere, moving, and encouraging.

Kevin is **r**esponsible. I especially admire that trait about him. When he says that he is going to do something, you can consider it done.

Kevin is **o**ptimistic. Life has not always been a bowl of cherries for Kevin. He has overcome obstacles that most of us will never have to face. He lives life to the fullest.

The Hero Effect is about a man who overcame the heartbreak of a broken childhood, homelessness, and helplessness to become a person of amazing influence.

I am grateful for Kevin's message of hope. His words will help encourage, inspire, and motivate you to become the person you want to be.

Finally, this is a book that you will want to share with someone who needs a hero in his or her life. Enjoy Kevin's message just like you would savor an extra-large plate of apple pancakes covered in warm syrup. It is that good.

Then, pass it on.

David Cottrell
Author, *Monday Morning Leadership*
Boerne, Texas

Table of Contents

The World Needs Heroes

The world needs heroes. I don't mean people running around wearing tights and a cape. (Unless you're into that.) The world needs heroes who are just like you. Everyday people in ordinary roles who have the extraordinary capacity to make a profound difference right where they are. The heroes around you may be disguised as:

+ People who consider it a privilege to lead, love, and serve others.

+ People who go out of their way to help others dream big dreams, achieve great things, and leave us better than they found us.

+ People who exceed our expectations, and when they commit to doing something, we can confidently consider it done.

✦ Those who make even the harshest critics marvel at how they consistently show up and make a positive difference at work and in life.

The world needs heroes:

✦ Brave ones who achieve the impossible in spite of the odds. Those who dare to act and bring forth results that were invisible to everyone else.

✦ Strong ones who help shoulder the load when life gets hard. Heroes who breathe life into those who can't seem to catch their breath.

✦ Brilliant ones who create, innovate, and make life easier—those who draw upon their unique talent and skills to provide hope to the hopeless.

The world needs heroes who are innovators and entrepreneurs, problem solvers, and healthcare providers. Heroes who are teachers, pastors, defenders and protectors of freedom, and the very best in their chosen profession.

The world needs heroes all around us, and you need heroes all around you. Heroes who are willing to bring their best to the present moment and pour it into the lives of others. The heroes who show up when it matters the most and inspire, motivate, and equip us for this journey we are all taking together. We need heroes who will help clarify our mind, purify our heart, and edify our soul.

This book is about what happens when extraordinary people show up and choose not to be ordinary. After all, you weren't created for an ordinary life. Regardless of your title or position, you have an effect on all those around you. You have an opportunity to be a hero. You can be your best when it matters the most.

This book is designed to inspire and equip you to become a hero to those around you. It is not for those who believe they are entitled to something or anything. Nor is it for those who are satisfied with the status quo.

It is for those who want to break through and enjoy being a hero right where you are. The people around you need heroes. You, indeed, can be that person.

Read and apply ***The Hero Effect*** and learn how to be your best when it matters the most.

The Hero Effect

chapter 1

My Quest for Heroes Started with a Question

My quest for heroes began one day while preparing a speech … one that was borne out of a conversation with a friend about what it means to be a hero. The keynote would be presented to a large group of people who would jam into a room to hear me deliver a speech I didn't yet have.

I stared at my yellow pad. It had one word scribbled, underlined, and circled on it:

My task was to deliver a motivational talk to this organization. The audience would be people who worked for a world-class organization—the best in their industry. They were a hard-working, experienced team that helped people put their lives back together in the wake of disasters big and small.

I knew the audience well. After all, I had spent nearly two decades working alongside them.

They are family to me.

The word "hero" was often used by their customers in describing their experience with this amazing team of people. Hero represented an attitude, a result of the quiet confidence that permeated throughout the organization. I wanted to honor the heroic efforts they put forth every day. I wanted them to know how important they are and that the work they do matters.

I had given talks before but never anything like this. I had delivered typical run-of-the-mill executive speeches. You know the kind: leadership, vision, communication, and customer service, the types of speeches many of us have experienced in business meetings and training programs.

This was different.

How was I going to talk about what it meant to be a hero at work and in life? What did I have to say about that?

Panic began to set in. I was concerned that I would not be able to inspire the people who made a living inspiring others … real heroes. I was a little freaked out.

When I begin to freak out, I go to my inner circle—the people who unconditionally know, love, and support me. The core of my inner circle is my wife, Lisa. When I married Lisa more than twenty years ago, I "married way up." She is gorgeous on the outside and equally as beautiful on the inside. She is the most positive person I know, and I love her more than anything else on the planet. She is incredible and one of my biggest heroes.

I asked Lisa what I should do. I explained that I was stuck preparing for this hero speech and didn't know where to begin.

Lisa has a loving way of calming me and getting me to focus on the task at hand. She could tell that I was nervous about this speech and she wanted to help. She sat down with me, took me by the hands and said, "You are overthinking this talk. When you get on that stage, just tell your story. Tell those people about your life."

She paused, smiled, and then added, "Everyone can learn from failure, poor decisions, and bad judgment. Besides, everybody feels better about their life once they've heard about yours."

Her words made me chuckle. And then I thought, "I still love her, but she is no longer part of my inner circle."

I'm kidding, of course. She is the foundation of my inner circle.

Her words kept bouncing around in my head: "Just tell your story…"

I went back to her and said, "Help me understand. How does that help me talk about heroes?"

The Faces in the Mirror

Lisa looked directly at me and said, "Let me explain it this way. When you look in the mirror, do you see yourself or all the people who helped you become you? Do you see the people who helped you when you couldn't help yourself? How about the people who picked you up when life knocked you down? Do you see the people who loved you even when you were unlovable?"

She continued, "If you don't see those faces, then you are missing the picture completely. You know that you are not a self-made man. You are the sum total and the byproduct of everyone who has ever shown up in your life. Think about all the people who have stopped by and poured a little bit of themselves into you—leaving you better than they found you. Some were there for a moment and some for a lifetime. If you want to talk about heroes, you know plenty of them. That would be a good place to start."

Lisa was exactly right. No one gets anywhere on his or her own. We all need help moving from where we are to someplace new. We need help getting to our next level. We need help becoming more of who we were born to be.

People flow in and out of our lives, some for a minute and some for a lifetime. Some appear discreetly, while some get in your face. Some are by your side while others are in the background. Regardless of how they appear, we all have heroes.

I raced back to my yellow pad, turned to a clean sheet, and wrote a question across the top: *What does a hero look like?*

BECOMING A HERO

Look around. Who are your heroes? Who are the faces in the mirror that you reflect? Do they know that they are your heroes? Do they know that they make a positive difference in your life? If not, now is a good time to tell them.

Look around, again. Who do you see that needs a hero?

I once heard a story about Muhammad Ali. He was on a plane that began experiencing turbulence. The flight attendant asked him to fasten his seat belt. Ali quipped, "Superman doesn't need a seat belt." The flight attendant fired right back, "Superman doesn't need an airplane, either. Please fasten your seat belt."

People around you will need your help during their times of turbulence. You may be the one to tell them to "fasten their seat belt." You may have to fasten the seat belt for them. Or, you may be able to point out where their seat belt is located.

You can be their hero.

chapter 2

What Does a Hero Look Like?

"What does a hero look like?" Those words loomed large on the fresh sheet of yellow paper. I sat and pondered, thinking about what Lisa had said. I closed my eyes, visualizing the people who had helped me along the way.

I rose from my desk and went to a mirror that was nearby. I stood in front of it and stared at myself for an uncomfortable amount of time. Minutes ticked by. The image of my face began to fade.

Crystallizing before me were the faces of my heroes. I saw my parents. I saw my teachers and preachers, friends, and family. I saw co-workers and colleagues and even the faces of a few people I barely knew at all, but they had made a difference in my life.

With these portraits foremost in my mind, I went back to my yellow pad and pondered the question that was begging for an answer.

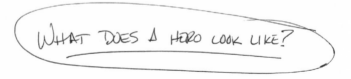

WHAT DOES A HERO LOOK LIKE?

I was stuck. How do you define such a group of people? All of them are different. They each have a special quality about them. Every one of them has made their own unique contribution to my life. What was the common thread?

How do you define the word "hero"?

I needed some help. I grabbed a pad and pencil and set out to pose that question to everyone I knew and some people I had never seen before. I wanted to know how others define the idea of being a hero. I asked friends, neighbors, people in airports … everywhere I went, I asked random people what a hero looks like.

The Gold Standard

A common example of a hero revealed in my unscientific study was our military personnel, the defenders and protectors of our freedom. The ones who sacrifice for people whom they will never meet, faces they will never see, and names they will never know. These brave men and women are the real deal when it comes to the business of being a hero. They are the gold standard in the hero world.

And most of the time, they are invisible. They blend in virtually unnoticed by the people they serve. Don't you think they deserve to be treated like heroes? I do.

Unconditional Heroes

Chad is one of my best friends who is also married to a wonderful lady named Lisa. She believes that our military heroes should be treated like heroes. She is the most patriotic person I have known. When she sees men or women in uniform, she is going to hug them, love them, thank them, and, if she is anywhere near food, she will buy them a meal.

Almost every Friday evening, the four of us go out for dinner. Recently we were eating in a local Cracker Barrel restaurant. We were sitting, talking, and having a good time when through the door came a guy wearing fatigues. The three of us looked at each other and grinned. We knew exactly what was about to happen.

The hostess seated the guy a couple of tables over from us. Sure enough, before we could blink, Chad's Lisa was on the move. She made her way over to his table and sat down across from him. He was totally surprised and shocked.

He pushed himself back from the table. Lisa then reached across the table, grabbed his hands, and pulled him close. She said, "Sir, I just want to thank you for your service to our country. I want to thank you for going to work every day to keep us safe and keep us free. Thank you for keeping my boys safe. I have two of them. Thank you for keeping my dogs safe. I have two of them, Shelties. Thank you for keeping my husband safe. I have just one of those."

And it's always in that order: the boys, the dogs, then Chad.

This guy was stunned. He was wide-eyed and speechless.

Lisa wasn't finished. She leaned in and said, "Sir, it would be my honor to buy your meal as a small token of appreciation for all that you do."

The guy let go of her hands, leaned back, and with a sheepish grin and a deep southern drawl said, "Aw, ma'am, I'm not in the military. I've just been out hunting."

She turned three shades of red and came back to the table. We cracked up and did what any good group of friends would do: we laughed. We imitated the hunter's voice and made the same gestures. After several minutes, Lisa had enough. Chad knew it was time to knock it off or the rest of his night wasn't going to be much fun. He said something to her that was absolutely profound. What he said is a relevant starting place for a dialogue about heroes.

He looked at his bride and said, "Lisa, you can never go wrong doing the right thing."

Those are powerful words. You can never go wrong treating someone with kindness and respect. Not because there is something in it for you, but because it is the right thing to do.

Okay, so we bought a hunter his meal that night. Is that such a bad thing? In fact, if you're ever in Nashville, throw on some hunting gear and head over to the Cracker Barrel. We may see you there.

I believe that many people have strayed from the basics of kindness and human decency. It appears to me that we live in a society where people have become indifferent, even blind to one another. It's as if we need to be rewarded to muster up kindness. It seems as though everyone is only concerned about "What's in it for me?"

Many people go through life based on conditions: "I will do this for you if you do this for me." We hold each other to the letter of the contract. Every encounter is a transaction or negotiation.

Heroes don't think about conditions. Heroes think like Chad's Lisa. She stood up, approached her hero … even though her hero was just a guy who happened to go hunting that day … she made a move to express her kindness and gratitude. Was that a bad move?

What Makes the Great Ones Great?

Armed with my one question and a yellow pad, I continued my quest to answer what a hero looks like. I wanted to know the qualities and characteristics of a hero. Why do we pull certain people out of the pile and place them on a pedestal?

As I kept asking the question, people would talk about all the "categories" of heroes in their world. They talked about world changers like Nelson Mandela, Martin

Luther King Jr., and Mother Teresa. They spoke of first responders and caregivers. They mentioned the doctors and nurses who nurture and heal us when we are broken. I heard stories of teachers, tutors, and the coach who made all the difference in a young life, as well as the neighbor, the friend, or the stranger who helped in a moment of need.

Some were singing the praises of their favorite sports heroes. They would tell how the great ones can play the same game just like everyone else but at a level that made it an art form unto itself.

They talked about great brands they buy and how they love to spend their money with companies that exceed their expectations and offer an experience they don't receive anywhere else.

As I continued to ask more people the question, a pattern began to develop. I must have asked two hundred people the question: "What does a hero look like?" Regardless of where I was or whom I was asking, I kept hearing the same words: Heroes are ordinary people who do extraordinary things.

At first, it sounded right. I thought that was absolutely the definition we have placed upon heroes in our society.

Turn on the news or read the newspaper, and you will most certainly hear similar words to describe a hero.

After hearing it over and over again, I began to wonder, *Is that really true?* Are heroes really just ordinary people doing extraordinary things, or have we been conditioned to think about heroes in the wrong way? Have we been convinced that somehow we were all born ordinary and are destined to spend our lives living as ordinary people with only the occasional burst of extraordinary?

Born Extraordinary

The thought came to me that maybe we were all born extraordinary and we made choices to become ordinary somewhere along the way. Could that be true?

Looking at it from the beginning, the day you were conceived, a miracle occurred. Science tells us that when you were dropped off at the pool, there were around a hundred million other kids dropped off that same day. One hundred million applicants for the job of being you. Only you got through.

You started working, paddling your way through the crowd. Out of the shallow end and into the wide-open ocean of possibility. Wearing your tiny cap and goggles, you started moving, and all of a sudden, you hit your stride. Like a little Michael Phelps swimming for gold, you crossed the finish line first. You made it through. You beat the odds. You became the miracle. And nine months later, you received your gold medal: the gift of an unblemished canvas on which to paint the story of your life.

That sounds pretty extraordinary to me. Created in the image of perfection. A miracle at birth, endowed with the talents, gifts, and abilities that are as unique as your fingerprints. There's nothing ordinary about that. Perhaps we've had it wrong the whole time. Perhaps we've been conditioned to think about heroes in the wrong way, leaving us to believe that it's okay to be ordinary most of the time and, only occasionally, let our extraordinary selves shine through.

Ordinary Is a Choice

I began thinking that maybe ordinary is a choice that prevents extraordinary people from becoming their best. It suppresses greatness and fosters a false sense of averageness that manifests itself as a lifetime of mediocrity. Could that be true?

What began to stir in me was this idea that the great ones think just the opposite of everyone else. The reason they are heroes is because they *think* and *act* differently.

They show up with their best stuff when it matters the most. They understand they were born extraordinary, and they show up every day and choose not to be ordinary. They are willing to do the hard work of putting in the time, effort, and mental focus to bring forth their extraordinary gifts. Their habits are extraordinary.

Unfortunately, far too many people go through life as miniature versions of all they could have been. Intentionally stunted by their own hand to be less than they were created to be.

Many ordinary people do a little bit of work, and if they don't see results, move on and start all over again someplace else. They find another new opportunity and attempt to put down roots, only to become frustrated too soon and give up again. They are in a constant state of stopping and starting. They want instant gratification and are too impatient to do the hard work of realizing their true potential. They were created to achieve some measure of success. Instead they remain content to live in their own comfort zone and they quit before they achieve their breakthrough.

Here is what I have discovered: It takes just as much work to be a small, ordinary version of yourself as it does to be the giant, extraordinary version you were born to be.

Do yourself and the world a favor and choose to be better than ordinary.

Why Ordinary People are Ordinary

One person I talked to and asked what a hero looked like was a ten-year-old version of myself. Kids have a brilliant way of seeing themselves and the world. They are confident. They think they showed up with all the right stuff. They believe they are here to save the world and make a positive impact.

Adulthood has a way of squeezing that confidence and certainty out of us. We get wrapped up in life, and somewhere along the way, we become convinced that there's nothing special about us. We become content to just get by, accomplishing the bare minimum. We tell ourselves—and others—not to make waves, we're living the dream, when all we're doing is simply trying to survive.

Yet the only people who have ever done anything significant were the people who did more than just get by. They raised their hands when the game was on the line and shouted, "Put me in, coach!" They made some waves. "Getting by" wasn't part of their vocabulary. "Live fully and thrive" is their mantra.

When I was a kid, I wanted to be Superman. I thought it was a job you could get. I thought I had superpowers and could change the world. I thought I had something extra and was destined for greatness. I even thought I could fly and would tie a bath towel around my neck and run through the house, jumping off furniture. It drove my mother crazy. (My wife doesn't like it, either.)

One day I had my cape on. It was working well. Flying with ease, I ran through the house, jumping off furniture. First, the couch. I jumped and flew three feet. Then I climbed the kitchen cabinets next to the refrigerator. I took a deep breath and jumped. This time I flew five feet.

I was feeling confident, so I went outside and climbed the tree next to our garage and got onto the roof of the garage. I walked to the edge of the roof and stared at the driveway below. I had confidence and trusted the cape to do its job.

I took a deep breath and, with outstretched arms, I jumped. I flew straight down and landed on the pavement with a thud. My lip started to quiver. I could feel tears welling up in my eyes. "Superman doesn't cry," I said quietly to myself while holding my knee. My mom heard the commotion and, in one superhuman leap, swooped in to rescue her baby boy. She picked me up, dusted me off, checked me for bruises, and kissed me on the forehead. And then she scolded me like I had never been scolded before.

From that moment on, Superman was grounded.

When we were kids, we looked at the world differently. We believed in something bigger than ourselves. We could close our eyes and escape to a place where not even the sky was the limit. As we mature, our experiences and knowledge change our perspective and choices. We can no longer fly with a cape, but we can still be a superhero.

Heroes Transform the Ordinary

In my neighborhood, the kids lived for the day when someone bought a washer, dryer, or refrigerator so we could play with and decorate the box that the appliance came in. Limited only by the boundaries of our imagination, that box represented anything we wanted it to be: a race car, an army fort, a spaceship. We would decorate the box. Our imagination would transport us from where we were to someplace better. Someplace new.

Then, we grew up. We begin pruning that kid out of our life, stunting our creativity, and leaving ourselves inside the box that we live and do business in. The older we got, the more confined, conformed, and defined we became by the box we were living in.

The box is nothing more than the rules of the game. It's the policies, procedures, systems, and people that make up our world. Every arena of endeavor has its rules: a box where the players reside and the game is played. For some, it's a field or a court. For others, an office or a cube. For some, it's their home or the open road.

Regardless of the box, heroes show up every day, limited only by their imagination. They decorate their box. They paint with broad strokes of talent and ability to create a masterpiece on the canvas of their life. They play the same game as everyone else, but when they show up to do what they do, it looks special. It looks different than the game everyone else is playing, even though they are subject to the same rules as everyone else. They don't conform to the box, instead they transform the box. They bend, shape, twist, and color the box in a way that makes it into something new. The box becomes a canvas upon which to paint their next masterpiece.

Maybe it is time for you to take the box that you are living in and transform it. Heroes live by the rules but maintain their imagination and creativity to transform their ordinary, mundane box into a brilliant, fun, productive use of the box that they have been given.

Reimagining Heroes

Heroes choose to be extraordinary every day, all day. If you do not believe that, you accept the idea that heroes are ordinary people who occasionally do extraordinary things. You would also be giving yourself permission to be average and mediocre when it is convenient for you. You may occasionally allow your extraordinary self to show up and do great things. When you make the choice of being ordinary, you must first convince yourself that you aren't anything special. You have to tell yourself over and over again that you have no reason for being anything other than ordinary, which is not true. You can choose to be extraordinary; that is your most natural choice. You must lie to yourself in order to sell yourself on the idea that you are just ordinary.

I believe the people whom we label as heroes think very differently than everyone else. They are clear about the responsibility that comes with greatness. They know beyond a shadow of a doubt that they were born with talents, gifts, and abilities that are unique to them and endowed with the potential to impact the world by using their passion to serve others well. I believe they show up every day with the intent of being their very best.

Let's reimagine this idea of being a hero. Instead of an ordinary person who does something extraordinary, let's redefine what it really means to be a hero.

A hero is an extraordinary person who chooses not to be ordinary.

If you buy into the notion that everybody was born extraordinary, then you must concede that ordinary thinking is a learned behavior, a conditioned response based on the voices in our head. You have been convinced of your unworthiness. Your averageness shows up in the way you talk to yourself and to others. You become stuck thinking, "I am not good enough." "It will never work out." "It just wasn't meant to be." Or my favorite: "I am who I am." No, you're not. You are who you decide to become, and it begins with understanding and believing that you were born extraordinary. If you become ordinary, it will be your choice.

You can make the choice to be extraordinary right where you are and become a hero for those around you.

BECOMING A HERO

What does a hero look like to you?

Are your heroes invisible? Do they go unnoticed, disguised as just another person? Maybe it is time to pay attention to the heroes around you.

Do you have the courage to confront and acknowledge heroes like Lisa did, even if you may feel foolish if you make a mistake?

What box are you living in that is restricting your creativity and growth?

What if you asked yourself, "Is the choice that I am making going to help me become ordinary or extraordinary?"

What can you begin doing today to become a hero for those around you?

chapter 3

The Fantastic Four Qualities of a Hero

Armed with my new paradigm, I began to look for the everyday heroes in my world. I wanted to know what heroism looks like. Why do I gravitate to certain people? How do they perform at a consistently high level and make me stop in my tracks and admire their work?

I soon realized that heroes do certain things better than everyone else. They show up with a different mindset and focus. Specifically, I noticed four fantastic qualities that are evident every time a hero shows up.

1. Heroes *help* people—with no strings attached.

2. Heroes create an *exceptional* experience for the people they serve.

3. Heroes take *responsibility* for their attitude, their actions, and their results.

4. Heroes see life through the lens of *optimism*.

Each of these qualities seems so simple, don't they? However, if you were to be a champion of all four of these simple qualities, you would be a hero to everyone around you. That is a choice that you can make, starting now.

Let's take a closer look at each one of these four qualities of a hero.

1 Heroes *help* people ... with no strings attached

The first thing I began to notice about heroes in my life is that heroes help people. On the surface, there is nothing profound or revolutionary about that idea, and you may not be scrambling to find a highlighter right now. In fact, you may have just rolled your eyes. If you did, I get it. But stay with me for a minute.

Everyone comprehends that heroes help people. We understand on some level that helping others is a key ingredient to success in life. We have heard from many sources that serving others is the pathway to making a difference and creating wealth. Yet, even though we are taught this idea of servanthood, it has been my experience that most people actually don't get it.

I have observed that most people try to be helpful to the extent that it's worth *their* anticipated return on investment. They evaluate if it is worth their time and attention to give something more for a greater something in return. In other words, there is a motive. There's quid pro quo. It is conditional upon another person's action. Many people bargain, negotiate, and work an angle to get what they want. Heroes don't do that.

What I discovered as I dug into this idea of helping others is that there is another piece—more than just helping—that heroes execute instinctively. I noticed that the heroes in everyday life have reached a higher level in the area of serving others.

Heroes have mastered the dot, dot, dot. What's the dot, dot, dot? It's the something extra that sets them apart. Heroes not only help people, but—dot, dot, dot—they do so with no strings attached.

Heroes help people … with *no strings attached*. No pretense. No conditions. No agreement. No contingencies.

Sometimes the "no strings attached" rubs our humanness the wrong way. We are wired to live by the letter of the law, the contract rules. The transaction drives behavior. We think in terms of, "I will do this for you, if you do this for me." One of our greatest battles in becoming a hero is the fight to suppress our humanness and embrace our humanity.

Heroes approach their work and their life very differently. They bring a passion and a focus on the outcome for their customer, student, co-worker, and friend that is different from almost everyone else. They are not caught up in transacting business. They are deeply caught up, however, in transforming moments and leaving the people they serve wanting more.

Heroes step up and deliver excellence every single time, and because of this, their fans evangelize their story to the rest of the world. In business, they drive new customers and more business to heroes again and again and again.

You can become a dot, dot, dot master. You can become the hero whom people yearn to be around because they know that you operate with a "no strings attached" mindset.

2 Heroes create an *exceptional* experience for the people they serve

One of my heroes is my hairstylist, Rebekah. She is a dot, dot, dot master who creates an exceptional experience.

To provide some background: I've had bad hair my whole life. People who hold advanced degrees in hair care have told me since I was a kid that my hair is difficult to cut. It has a mind of its own, and the texture falls somewhere between barbed wire and straw.

Having bad hair is one thing. Paying to receive bad haircuts is another matter entirely. Trust me, it's not a good combination.

Before I met Rebekah, I was on a roll of bad haircuts. For more than a year, I tried salon after salon. I would come home after every haircut and complain to my wife, Lisa.

After a year of my moaning, Lisa had all she could handle. She took matters into her own hands. She called her stylist, obtained a referral, made my appointment, and told me where to go.

When I showed up at the recommended hair salon, it was packed. People filled the waiting area. Hair was flying everywhere. This place was busy.

As I stood there, a young lady in the back of the salon—a vivacious brunette with big blue eyes—noticed me. She flashed a giant smile and started walking toward me with an outstretched hand. She shook my hand and said, "My name is Rebekah. You must be Kevin." Caught off guard, I asked, "How did you know?" She smiled and replied, "Your wife described your haircut!"

I gave a half-hearted smile and sat down in her chair. Immediately she began asking about me. She asked about my life, how long I'd been married, and if we had kids. She asked about my work and if I was any good at it. We laughed and told stories. You would have never guessed we had just met.

Rebekah drew me in with a smile, but she kept my interest because she had mastered the dot, dot, dot.

We were laughing and talking when Rebekah began massaging my neck and shoulders. As tension melted away, I found myself beginning to relax, which was far too uncommon in my fast-paced, stressed-out life. Every person's role is to solve problems. In fact, the degree to which you can help solve other people's problems can determine to a large extent your own happiness, wealth, and future opportunities.

Rebekah was focused. She never texted, tweeted, or posted anything while I was in her chair. She didn't talk to the person to her right or left. She stayed focused on me the entire time. It was like I was the only person in her world at that moment in time.

I walked into her salon for a haircut. Rebekah worked magic while cutting my hair. She paid attention to me. She laughed with me. I had a great time.

When she put her scissors down, she stepped back and gave me a good look up and down. She nodded her approval and smiled. As she pulled the cape from around my neck, she slowly spun the chair so I faced the mirror. As soon as I saw myself in the mirror, she said: "There you go, Mr. Delicious!"

I blushed. Mr. Delicious? No one has ever called me Mr. Delicious. I was stunned. I felt good about myself. The haircut was secondary. She noticed me. She validated me. She made me feel special.

Let's review: I am a middle-aged man. Nobody rubs my shoulders. In fact, I asked her about it, and her response blew me away. She said, "I do that for everyone. It's my way of removing some of the stress and tension that people have in their life. Doing business with someone should not be stressful."

Nobody cuts my hair like Rebekah. No one has *ever* called me Mr. Delicious. I asked Rebekah if she calls all of her customers "Mr. Delicious." She said, "Nope. Just you." And I believe her. Since my first visit with Rebekah, I have asked my team, my wife, and my friends to call me Mr. Delicious. So far that request has been denied 100 percent of the time.

Some of you may be thinking: Does giving someone a haircut really make them a hero? Yes. It does. If you understand that the role of a hero is to relieve stress and solve problems. She relieved my stress and solved my problem. She made my life better.

Heroes make life better. They simplify things and are easy to do business with. Heroes know that the easier it is to do business with them, the harder it is for the competition to take their customers. Heroes dominate the emotional space between their customer's head and their heart. They know that if they make an emotional connection, people will fight to find the logic to support their decision to do business with you.

This is profoundly relevant. I am not suggesting you call your customers and clients "Mr. or Mrs. Delicious." That would be weird. And, just to be clear, the name is already taken. I drive by at least twenty salons to get to Rebekah's, and most of these salons are cheaper. Saving a couple of dollars doesn't matter. Rebekah's dot, dot, dot exceptional service is worth going out of my way to invest my time and money with someone who is amazing at their job. That is what I want for my business, and it's what I want for my personal life with my friends and family: to be the only choice; to be the obvious choice. Isn't that what you want?

The Non-negotiables

Rebekah's operating philosophy starts with a non-negotiable mindset. The playbook for how she decided to run her life begins with a foundation of how she *chooses* to treat people. For her, it's non-negotiable. This is a common thread with heroes. They treat people right, own the moments that matter, and they know that every moment matters.

The agreement with Rebekah is simple. I exchange money for a haircut. That's our deal. She transcended our agreement by making a personal connection. Now, we have adopted Rebekah into our own family, and when you do business with family, it changes everything. You not only give them your loyalty, you give them grace. You forgive them when they occasionally drop the ball or make a mistake.

Many people and organizations operate from a transactional perspective, meaning they are focused on the conditions of the contract: "I will do this for you, if you do this for me." Their covenant is to perform the minimum required to get by.

They focus on things that are not really important, such as making excuses, or the busywork and fake priorities we come up with that keep them from creating an above-and-beyond experience for those they serve. The non-essentials are *anything* that doesn't move your priorities forward. It's anything that distracts and detracts you from bringing your best stuff to the present moment and pouring it into the lives of others.

Heroes think differently. They aren't focused on conditions. Heroes are focused on connections. Heroes reach beyond what is required to achieve the remarkable. They begin with a philosophy of how they will treat others. Their foundation is rooted in the non-negotiable, while others are focused on non-essentials.

The number one thing that keeps you from being your best is your *decision to be ordinary*. Deciding to show up and be like everyone else. Deciding to do the minimum required to get by.

If you want to be your very best, then decide on your non-negotiable. What do you stand for? Decide what will not be compromised in your life. Decide how others will define their experience with you. Decide your own operational philosophy for life that will reach beyond your professional life and into everything you do.

A non-negotiable mindset deals in absolutes—the things that won't be compromised—there is no bending or flexing. The things that you refuse to sacrifice at any price.

For Rebekah, it was simple. When it comes to how she treats people, she is unwavering. She takes a personal interest in her clients and demonstrates a caring attitude. She then delivers more than anyone expected, exceeding expectations in every way.

Rebekah is a shining example of what it means to transcend the conditions of the relationship and create a connection that changes everything. She is not wrapped around the axle of transacting business. Rebekah is in the business of transforming the encounter completely and, in the process, creates raving friends and fanatical followers who tell her story for her. That's how you build your personal and professional brand.

3 Heroes take *responsibility* for their attitude, their actions, and results

There's a motivational quote that says, "If it is to be, it is up to me!" How true it is.

Unfortunately, many people have modified that quote to say, "If it is to be, don't look at me!" Average people are content to move their own integrity outside of their responsibility. They look to the people around them and point the finger. They blame leadership. They spend more time looking for the reasons they can't get it done and zero time figuring out how to make it happen. To them, it is everyone else's fault that they can't achieve better results. They convince themselves and work tirelessly to convince everyone else that they work harder than everyone around them. They will gladly tell you they are more committed than everyone else. They say they are overwhelmed and have too much work to do, more than any five people could possibly get done.

Heroes act differently. Heroes are the epitome of what it means to take responsibility for their results. They own the moment and know that every moment matters. They spend their time looking for ways to make it happen and produce the best possible outcome for the people they serve.

Heroes hold themselves to a standard that no one else would even expect. Every day they get better and more capable. They are focused on how they can improve their performance and, in so doing, make everyone around them better.

Heroes take responsibility and lead by example.

4 Heroes see life through the lens of *optimism*

Optimism is different than positive thinking. People are afraid of the idea of being optimistic because they are afraid they will be labeled as some sort of positive-thinking freak.

For the record, I am not a positive thinker.

It seems reasonable that positive thinking is a prerequisite to become a motivational speaker. It is not. And while I am not a positive thinker, I am an optimist. Here's the difference: Positive thinkers are great pretenders. If they encounter a challenge, roadblock, or obstacle, they pretend that it doesn't exist. They believe if they ignore it, it might just disappear.

The optimist, on the other hand, encounters the same challenge, roadblock, or obstacle, and they face it head on. They don't pretend it doesn't exist. They acknowledge it as a problem that requires focus and attention to conquer.

My dad used to say, "Sometimes you're the windshield, and sometimes you're the bug." How true it is. You never know what life is going to throw in your path. Heroes are always prepared to deal with what comes their way.

I once took our family to see a movie called *A Bug's Life*, a 3-D movie. It was a good movie, but without the 3-D glasses, it was nothing but a big, blurry screen. We went to the afternoon matinee and, as we sat in our seats, we noticed another couple settling close by with their kids.

There was an argument taking place between mom and dad. Dad was saying, "I'm not putting on those stupid glasses." Mom replied, "You are putting on the glasses! We are here for the children!" With both arms in the air, Dad said, "I am not wearing these silly glasses. They are going to make me look like a dork!"

I leaned over to Lisa and whispered, "He should have thought about that before he strapped on his fanny pack. Too late!" I put my 3-D glasses on to conceal my identity at that point.

I think about that guy when I think about this idea of optimism. Many people are unwilling to wear the optimism glasses that have been given to them, which would make life more pleasant. They're afraid of what other people are going to think. They don't want to be singled out as "the positive-thinking freak." They let what other people think determine how they see and respond to the world.

Think about that for a minute. How often do you let someone else's opinion or perspective become your own? How often do you alter what you *know* you should do because of what someone else says, thinks, or does?

Heroes are comfortable in their own skin. They make their own decisions and consciously choose how they are going to show up. They act in spite of their fears and insecurities. They actually use them as catalysts to propel forward. They are unafraid to step outside their comfort zones.

It is time to put on your glasses of optimism. Optimism gives heroes a couple of secret weapons. First, it gives them supernatural vision. It allows them to see what others cannot see. They see their jobs, their families, their communities, and their lives in a new light. They see things not as they are but as they can be—people not as they are but as they can be. They see situations and circumstances not as they are but as they should be.

Second, optimism is the great equalizer. It helps us process information differently—to see what others see but apply it in a different way. Heroes use this power as leverage to stay one step ahead of everyone else and act in a manner that seems to give them a slight edge.

Life Without Murphy

Optimism changes your luck. It changes your perspective on things that happen in life. It allows you to rise above the things that hold most people down and provides you the wisdom to respond to situations rather than react to what happens.

I hear people talk about Murphy's Law, which basically says that whatever can go wrong, will go wrong and at the worst possible time. People who believe it wind up experiencing it. Most of the time it plays out exactly as they imagined.

For years, my wife and I joked about Murphy's Law. We believed the universe had placed a target on our backs and was out to get us. Every time we turned around, it seemed something was going wrong. We had developed a Murphy's Law mindset. We even thought about changing our name to Murphy Brown. We were absolutely convinced we couldn't catch a break. That somehow we were dealing with things that other people weren't.

The reality is that most of what we were dealing with was normal. It was just life. It's the kind of everyday things that drag people down and add to their stress. By themselves, these things are small. If you try to explain them to people, they will look at you and ask, "So, what's the problem?" The challenge is that life happens on top of work and kids and marriage and everything else we have to deal with—everyone demanding our attention and desperately needing something from us.

Heroes think differently.

Heroes are larger than life. I don't mean flamboyant or weird. I'm not talking about walking into a room with your arms raised and announcing, "Relax, everyone, I am here to save the day." For heroes, it's the opposite. A hero walks into a room and, through his or her attitude and actions, portrays that, "*I am here to serve today!*"

In order to serve others, heroes rise above the challenges and adversities of everyday life. They have conditioned themselves to be bigger than their problems. They lift themselves and others up and provide a new perspective.

Sometimes the best thing you can do is get a different view of the problem. You have probably heard the saying, "I can't see the forest for the trees." It's absolutely true. When you're in the thick of a crisis, you think it's only happening to you. A case of the "poor, pitiful me" syndrome seeps into your head. It becomes difficult to see anything good. It's tough to be optimistic and see solutions when you are focused on the problem.

Heroes flex their optimism muscle and begin to see what's possible instead of what's probable. They look for solutions instead of reasons that it can't be done. They learn how to look from above the fray where they can think, create, and decide on the things that are most important to move their highest priorities forward.

Good Morning America anchor Robin Roberts once said that optimism is "like a muscle: the more you use it, the stronger it gets." I believe that she is right. Rise up and take control. Optimism can take you places you've never dreamed of if you're willing to put on the glasses and see life as it was meant to be seen.

BECOMING A HERO

Heroes help people——with no strings attached——create an exceptional experience for the people they serve, take responsibility for the results, and see life through the lens of optimism.

Check yourself:

+ Do you make every person you come into contact with feel like they are the only person in the room?

+ What about the people who mean the most to you? Rabbi Shmuley Boteach puts it: "You are no hero if the people who mean the most to you think the least of you." What do those people think about you?

+ What "Rebekah" story would people tell about their experience with you?

+ How optimistic do you think you are? How optimistic do those around you think you are? Are you willing to make the choice to be more optimistic? Why not?

◆ What's holding you back from becoming a hero?

◆ What do you need to regain your perspective?

◆ What action can you take right now
   to move forward?

chapter 4

Josh-Brown

I want to share a story with you that will help paint a picture of how heroes show up at work and in life.

This story will demonstrate how pursuing your heroic qualities can revolutionize the way you see yourself and those around you. The lessons within the story exemplify the most important quality of a hero, and they have had a profound influence on my life.

The story is about my son. His name is Josh Brown. If you met him, he would tell you his name is "Josh-Brown." He thinks it's hyphenated, all one word.

When Josh was five years old, Lisa and I sat in a conference room with educators on one side of the table and doctors on the other. They were there to confirm what we suspected but were afraid to say out loud. We had known since he was three years old that his speech and language weren't developing as they should. On that day as we sat around a giant mahogany table, the educators and doctors would tell us that Josh had autism.

A doctor spoke first: "Mr. and Mrs. Brown, we are sorry to inform you that your son has autism. You need to prepare for the road ahead. This is going to be a long, hard journey for you and Josh. He won't learn like the other kids. He will be uneducable in some ways. It is not likely that he will graduate high school."

Tears dropped on the papers resting in Lisa's lap.

I was angry. I stopped listening. I began thinking about all the things Josh might not do. I am embarrassed to admit it, but the life I had hoped to live vicariously through my boy had just vanished. He wasn't going to be a star Little League shortstop or quarterback of the high-school football team. My dreams were smashed.

While I was feeling sorry for myself and thinking about all the things he wasn't going to do, Lisa was busy thinking otherwise. The tears disappeared, and a look of determination swept over her face. She began doing what great moms do: making things better.

When we returned home, Lisa didn't waste time thinking about everything he might not do. She was intensely focused on helping him achieve everything he was born to do. She went to work.

Lisa created a vision, plan, and strategy for our son's life. She set about attracting the right people to help our boy. She handpicked teachers, tutors, mentors, and coaches who showed up in our life one by one.

Like a magnet, she attracted friends, family, teachers, doctors, and sometimes even total strangers, to join us along this road. Some stayed for a minute; others have stayed by his side for years. Regardless of how long they stayed, each person played a role by providing Josh something he didn't have before they showed up. Each one poured a little bit of themselves into him and left

The Hero Effect

him better than they found him. They all have helped move him a little closer to his destiny.

It has been an incredible blessing and journey to be Josh-Brown's dad. He has taught me some of the most important lessons of my life, and because of him and the story I'm about to share, the trajectory of my life was forever changed.

Disney

When Josh was seven years old, he discovered Walt Disney World. For two years, Disney was all he could talk about. One common thread among kids with autism is that they tend to obsess. They become so singularly focused on their heart's desire that nothing else in the world exists. They have a difficult time letting things go. My wife, who is the most positive person I know, said that he was just "passionately encouraging us" to take a trip to Disney.

Lisa and I decided that when Josh turned nine years old, it would be a good time to take him to Disney. We had waited until we were sure he could thoroughly enjoy the trip and that it wasn't so overwhelming for any of us.

Vacations were more stressful than relaxing for me back then. I was a workaholic. I would come home from work and sit, present but unaccounted for, in my chair with the laptop open. I regarded a vacation as simply an excuse to work from somewhere other than the office. It took me years to learn to be present and accounted for, wherever I was. I cannot consistently perform at a high level if every time I show up I am thinking about someplace else I need to be or something else I need to be doing. I hope it does not take you as long as it took me to learn that lesson.

Making Magic

We were excited about our trip to Disney. We packed our bags and made a list. Josh-Brown checked the list constantly. I am not big on lists, but my wife and son are list people. Josh-Brown likes everything mapped out. No surprises. No guesswork.

Lisa's background is in accounting—she is very precise. She created an Excel spreadsheet detailing our entire trip. Everything we were going to do was spelled out by the minute. Every park, ride, and meet-and-greet was a line item on the grid for our trip to Disney.

With our list in hand, we took off for Orlando. Somehow we managed to arrive four hours ahead of our luggage, but that was no big deal. There's a lot to see and do at Disney, so we went exploring. It was a reconnaissance mission of sorts. We got the lay of the land to see how this was all going to play out for Josh-Brown's big adventure.

When we returned back to our room, our luggage finally joined us. We unpacked, settled in, and decided to go to bed, although no one was really sleepy. We were anxious to begin Josh-Brown's dream trip.

We all laid in bed, but no one was asleep. It reminded me of an old Disney commercial where they showed a little boy lying in bed the night before going to Disney. His eyes were closed, but he was awake. He was giggling under his breath. His mom whispered, "Honey, you have to go to sleep." The little boy, without opening his eyes, said, "But I'm so excited!"

All three of us felt like that little boy. Lisa and I were so excited for Josh-Brown that we could not sleep. We knew what this meant to him. We knew that, in his young mind, heaven must look a lot like Disney. Disney is a magical place. They have mastered the art of making you feel special by creating magical moments at every turn. And, it's especially magical because when you go there, your money disappears.

Apple Pancakes

Morning finally came. We woke up bright and early and ready to go.

I asked, "Josh-Brown, where are we eating breakfast?" He said, "Dad, we are eating downstairs in this hotel. We are going to ease you into this with no lines and no trams!" He is a smart boy and knows his father well.

Even though I had promised Lisa I wouldn't work on this trip, I couldn't help but pay attention to what was happening around me. As we headed down the escalator, I was fascinated by Disney's ability to create a culture where the "wow" factor is simply business as usual. We were in the customer-service and culture mecca of the universe. During our eight-day vacation, I was looking to learn the Disney customer-service "magic" so I could take it back and share with my clients.

I wanted to know how they created such magical and memorable experiences. How do they draw you in and make you feel so special? How do they get so much money out of your wallet and make you feel good about it? My radar was up. I paid attention.

We arrived at the restaurant where a cheerful hostess greeted us with a giant smile and said, "Welcome, Brown family! We are so glad you are here. We have a table just for you."

I made mental notes. With a giant smile, I thought, *That's cool. Brown family. Personalized, I like it. Table just for us. How special is that?*

She took us to our table. She gave us menus and said, "Brown family, may I be the first to wish you a magical day!" My thought bubble exploded as my jaw hit the table. A magical day? These people are good, really good.

The hostess left, and a waitress appeared. There was a different aura about our waitress. There was no giant smile or warm greeting. In fact, her expression suggested she was a little ticked off—or maybe just distracted. In a rushed tone and with eyes that hinted she would rather be anywhere but there, she said, "Can I get you something to drink?"

Lisa said, "Yes, however, I need to let you know my son is on a special diet. There are a lot of things he can have and a lot of things he can't have." Before Lisa could say another word, the waitress put her hand up as if to say, "Halt. Stop talking." She looked at Lisa and said, "I cannot take your order. You will need to speak to the executive chef." The waitress disappeared.

I have a boatload of money invested in this trip. I have high expectations. I expect people to smile, perhaps even whistle while they work. At the very least, I would appreciate it if they found it in their heart to hum "It's a Small World." I was a little ticked off by our waitress' attitude but decided not to say anything.

Bea
From the back of the restaurant we noticed the executive chef walking toward us. She was easy to spot wearing her crisp, white uniform with a Chef Boyardee hat. She approached our table. With a beautiful smile, she looked at Josh-Brown and said, "Good morning, Sunshine!"

Josh-Brown is really shy. He lowered his head and said, "Good morning."

The chef said, "My name is Bea. I understand we have someone on a special diet. How can I help?"

Lisa began to explain everything Josh could and couldn't eat. Bea pulled a notebook from her pocket and began to take notes on everything Lisa was telling her. Then Bea started asking questions. "How do you make that? What's in that? Where do you get that?" And the most important question: "What's his favorite?"

When she finished taking notes, she put the notebook away and turned to Josh-Brown. "Okay, Sunshine, what's for breakfast?" Josh lowered his head and asked for his favorite, "Apple pancakes, please."

Bea frowned a little and said, "Oh, Sunshine, I am so sorry. I don't have the ingredients to make your special kind of apple pancakes. Your mom told me how to make them. I just don't have the right ingredients. How about some bacon and eggs with some special toast just for you?"

Josh-Brown nodded and said, "Okay."

Bea left, and our waitress, Miss Personality, returned to take the rest of our order.

Our meal arrived and it was fine. We were satisfied but not impressed by our waitress. Few people notice when you simply deliver the basics and are just satisfied. It is not a "wow" experience when you do the minimum required to get by. Average service can be found almost anywhere you go. Even at Disney, the mecca of delivering a special "wow" service for their customers, my initial impression was created by the experience I had with the person who waited on our table.

There were heroes all around us, but we were blinded by the one person who may have had a bad day that day.

BECOMING A HERO

Heroes take responsibility for their actions and their results. Lisa was a hero when she took control of creating a plan to make Josh's life the best it could be.

Bea was not able to deliver exactly what Josh-Brown wanted for breakfast that morning, but she was a hero to us anyway. She took the time to listen, understand, and take notes. She asked a question that heroes frequently ask: "How can I help?"

The waitress was not a hero that day. In the greatest environment for creating special experiences, she did just enough to satisfy her customers to get by.

Becoming a hero is being your very best every day. That is a choice you make.

chapter 5

Disney – Day Two

"Josh-Brown, where are we eating breakfast?"

"Dad, I want to go see Aunt Bea!"

"Who?" I looked at Lisa with a confused look. She said, "The executive chef. Her name is Bea."

I asked Josh, "Buddy, what about our spreadsheet?" He responded with just a hint of attitude, "Dad, I want to go see Aunt Bea!"

Josh overrode the plan on the spreadsheet and we headed downstairs. When we arrived at the restaurant, our hostess greeted us with a big smile. "Welcome back, Brown family. No reservation today? That is not a problem. We have a table just for you." I thought, *I'm sure you do.*

She took us to exactly the same table where we sat the day before. Guess who was working our section? Miss Personality, of course. She still wasn't smiling. Maybe someone forgot to tell her she works at "the happiest place on earth." When she saw us arrive at one of her tables, she didn't even come to us. She immediately turned and walked toward the kitchen. Almost immediately from the kitchen emerged Aunt Bea. She was making a "Bea-line" to our table.

With her trademark smile, she turned to Josh-Brown and said, "Good morning, Sunshine!" He lowered his head and said, "Good morning."

"What's for breakfast, Sunshine?"

"Apple pancakes, please!"

"You got it, my dear. No problem."

I was stunned. I assumed that she had forgotten about Josh's special diet. I said, "Time out, Aunt Bea. Do you remember us from yesterday?"

"Yes, sir. I do."

"Aunt Bea, yesterday you didn't have the ingredients to make apple pancakes."

"Sir, why are you calling me Aunt Bea?"

"That's a fair question. Sorry. But yesterday you didn't have the ingredients."

"True."

"Today you do?"

"Yes."

"Where did you get them?"

"The store."

"Oh. So you sent someone to the store?"

"No, sir. I stopped on my way home. We have them all over Florida. Anyone can go."

I looked at her in amazement. I was shocked by what I had just heard. Nobody had ever done anything like this for us. I asked her perhaps the dumbest question I have ever asked anyone. I said, "Bea, that is very kind of you. Why would you do that?"

Her answer floored me. "I thought he wanted apple pancakes." Wow. How innovative. Do whatever it takes to make the customer happy. Or, in this case, do whatever it takes to blow the customer's mind and create loyalty for life. Right there the Brown family became fans of Aunt Bea and Disney for life.

After a few minutes, apple pancakes shaped like mouse ears were served to my son. I have never seen Josh-Brown smile the way he smiled that day. For the next six mornings, we abandoned the spreadsheet and Josh-Brown ate Aunt Bea's apple pancakes.

Heroes reach beyond what is required to achieve the remarkable. Bea certainly did that. Bea did more than she had to do. She created an exceptional, heroic experience.

When our vacation was over, we bought a thank-you card. Josh-Brown signed it, and Lisa and I put money in it and left it for Bea. Then, when we returned home, we wrote her bosses a letter that raved about her. A few weeks later, we bought another card. Josh-Brown signed it; Lisa and I put more money in it and mailed it to Bea. Disney was still costing me a fortune, but the truth is, we were happy to pay a premium for over-the-top service. We will gladly lay out our hard-earned cash when someone works hard to earn our business.

In the absence of an outstanding experience, attitude, or commitment, organizations are reduced to competing solely on price. Heroes operate on a different level. Winning is not just having the lowest price ... unless there is no value. When the perceived value is high, the priority of the price is low. When the perceived value is low, the priority of the price is high.

Heroes Make Better Choices

Bea had a choice. She could own the moment and create the best possible outcome given the circumstances, or she could have simply said that Josh-Brown's desire wasn't her problem and moved on. Fortunately for us, she chose to make a positive difference.

During our visit at the Disney restaurant, we encountered two very distinct people. One served us in an extraordinary way. The other didn't care that we were even there, which makes an important point. The choice to be extraordinary and serve at a higher level is always a personal choice, regardless of whether you work in the best culture on the planet or not. Being extraordinary is your responsibility and your choice every day.

Heroes choose wisely. For with great power comes the enormous responsibility to develop yourself and use your gifts to change the people around you in some positive way.

BECOMING A HERO

Bea showed up with an extraordinary attitude of service. It was obvious her choice was to say "*no*" to being ordinary. She was intentional about doing whatever she had to do to serve our family well. She brought her best self to the present moment and poured it into our experience.

Let's take a closer look at the "Bea attitudes."

Bea Happy: The first thing we noticed about Bea was her smile. She had a genuine smile that lit up the room. The smile on her face formed long before she got to our table. It was honest, sincere, and authentic.

I'm sure Bea had things going on in her life, just like everyone else. You can bet she was dealing with family, work, and life stuff the same way we do. The difference was that we never knew it. Many people drag that garbage-thinking around and they not only let it weigh them down, but they dump it on everyone they come in contact with. They feel compelled to share how difficult their life is and how miserable they are. And the more they talk about it, the worse they feel. Whatever you focus on multiplies. That is how life works.

I know that everyone is not over-the-top positive. They claim that they weren't born with a positive gene. They aren't happy by nature. They believe the worst excuse known to man: "That's *just the way I am*." That is *not* the way you are. It is the way you *choose* to be. Even if it's not your nature to be happy, it is still your choice to be happy or to be miserable.

Bea Kind: Bea's kindness was real. She did not learn it from a script or manual. Her kindness was not manufactured kindness that people muster up when they stand to get something in return.

Bea took a personal interest in our story. She was kind to Josh-Brown and *listened* to what he said …

and what he didn't say. When he asked for apple pancakes, she could tell by his expression they were his favorite. She paid attention and made a decision before she ever left the table to do something special for him. It was an act of kindness that reached far beyond the requirements of her job. Bea was intentionally kind to my boy.

Bea Present: To make a positive difference, you have to be present. Heroes are not distracted by their devices, vices, or every crisis in their life. Devices pull us away from the present moment. Our vices preoccupy us and we rush through the present moment. Every crisis blows up the present moment, and we make it about us instead of the people we are supposed to be with.

Heroes are present and accounted for. They block out distractions and focus on the task at hand. They live fully in the moment. They understand that nothing is casual and that everything deserves their full attention and focus—not a glancing blow or half-hearted effort.

Bea Willing: Some people are simply not willing to be a hero. Some aren't willing to show up, much less show out. Some aren't willing to be present and own the moments that matter. Some aren't willing to embrace their gifts and use them to serve others. Some aren't willing to persist and overcome the obstacles to find the best possible outcome for the people they serve.

Bea was willing. She had a willing spirit. She was willing to go above and beyond. She was willing to see further than the obstacles and roadblocks she encountered and serve at a higher level. She was willing to find a way when others would say, "No way."

To create an exceptional experience for the people you serve, you must be willing to show up, show out, and deliver results, without exception, every single time.

Bea Extraordinary: You cannot deliver an extraordinary experience without embracing an extraordinary attitude. Excellence is the product of confidence, competence, and countenance.

You can show that you are extraordinary when you enter the room with confidence. You can exhibit extraordinary by the demeanor and charisma that you exude—confident that you can stand and deliver. Competent because you've done the work to master your craft. Your presence is unmistakable. You have the countenance of a hero, a quiet quality that tells everyone around you that everything is going to be all right.

Bea showed up with her extraordinary self and delivered an exceptional experience—and then some.

How do you show up?

chapter 6

Josh-Brown and
Aunt Bea Reunion

In May 2016, Lisa and I were invited to a high-school graduation ceremony. Hundreds of people packed an arena to watch nearly three hundred high-school seniors receive their diplomas.

We were seated with friends and family in the upper deck. The graduates began marching into the arena, striding to their seats in unison. They walked in a single file, wearing their caps and gowns.

We watched intently for one particular graduate. Standing nearly six-feet tall with his cap a little crooked, our boy appeared. When Josh reached his seat, he turned and looked for us in the upper

deck. When he finally spotted us, he gave a quick
nod and then turned back to face the stage.

One by one they called out the names. Finally, we
heard the name that we had been waiting to hear:
Joshua Douglas Brown. When Josh rose from his
chair, chills ran up and down my spine. The hair
on the back of my neck stood up. Tears began to
roll down my face. It was one of the most powerful
moments I had ever experienced.

When it was time to receive his diploma, Josh
began moving toward his principal. His back was
straight. His head was high and looking forward.
He steadied his cap and gave his gown a tug. He
grabbed the honors cords that were draped around
his neck. There was a bit of a swagger in the way he
moved. He stood a little taller than usual. Pride and
confidence poured out of him.

People in the audience cheered and clapped even
though they were told not to. A lot of those people
knew his name. Many of them were part of his
team that helped him get on that stage. There were
heroes all around that arena.

Lisa and I had made our way downstairs to meet
Josh as he walked off the stage. We could barely

steady our phones to take photos because of the tears streaming down our faces. As he walked down the stairs and came toward us, he walked directly to his mom and hugged her. As he should have. Without Lisa's vision and her ability to plant that vision in Josh, along with the belief that this was possible, we would have never been in that arena.

That moment reminded me of my father's advice when I was a boy. Whenever I struggled with the opinions of others or when someone told me I couldn't do something, my dad would always say, "It doesn't matter what anyone else *thinks*. All that matters is what you *believe*." Lisa instilled that belief in Josh.

The experts didn't think Josh-Brown would graduate. They didn't think he could learn at a high level. They didn't think he would go to college. They were wrong. They failed to consider what he believed to be true. And they most certainly didn't know what his mother believed.

Those experts weren't with Josh and Lisa for the late-night study sessions. They weren't present when Josh-Brown put his head in his hands and asked, "Why doesn't my brain work?" And, they weren't there when his mother leaned down and whispered in his ear, "Honey, your brain is just fine. Being special just takes a little more work!"

Reunion

When we returned home after graduation, Josh, Lisa, and I sat at the dinner table, staring at his diploma.

Josh smiled and said, "I did good, right?"

I said, "Man, you did better than good. Your mom and I are very proud of you. To reward you for this great achievement, we want to take you on a trip. Anywhere you want to go in the world. Dad's hoping for Australia, but you pick."

Without hesitation, he looked at me and said, "Dad, I want to go see Aunt Bea."

I tilted my head slightly while opening one eye and said, "You're kidding me."

He said, "Nope. I really want to go see Aunt Bea."

I said, okay, and told him that we would begin working on making Disney 2.0 happen. After a few days, we were able to reconnect with Aunt Bea.

Emails were exchanged and the perfect reunion was set.

In July of that year, we went back for another eight days at Walt Disney World.

On the first day of our reunion tour, we were to reconnect with our old friend Bea at Disney's Hollywood Studios. By then, Bea had been a Disney cast member for over twenty years. She had worked her way up the ranks and had influenced hundreds of employees in several restaurants on the Disney properties.

After a morning in the park, we started to make our way to Hollywood Studios for lunch and to eventually connect with Bea. When we arrived at the restaurant, hundreds of people were waiting outside. I wasn't sure what was going on. There appeared to be an unusual amount of people waiting to get in.

After several minutes, we finally reached the young man working the host stand.

"A table for lunch, please."

He said, "Sure thing. What name is the reservation under?"

I said, "We don't have a reservation."

He said, "Sir, I'm sorry. We are jam packed and have all these people waiting. It's a meet-and-greet day—Handy Manny is here! Without a reservation, I do not have a table for you right now."

I said, "We have to get in there. We are here to see Aunt—I mean Chef Bea!"

He said, "I'm sorry."

We walked away.

Immediately Josh started tapping my arm. This typically means he has something to say.

"Dad, Dad, what just happened?"

I turned and said, "We don't have a reservation, son."

He wrinkled his brow and said, "You need to do something, Dad."

I did what I always do when I don't know what to do: I looked at Lisa.

Lisa said, "You need to do something, Dad!"

I made my way back up to the host stand and pleaded with the young man.

"I will give you everything in my wallet. Name your price. I have to get in there!"

He said, "Sir, I can't make any promises. Let me check."

He returned a few minutes later with one of those restaurant pagers that has the lights on it. He said, "I can get you in, but it's going to be at least forty-five minutes. We don't have a table for you, and you won't get to eat, but you can say hello."

I said, "We will take it!"

He said, "I still need a name."

I said, "Tell Bea that it's Josh-Brown, and he is here for apple pancakes!"

He grinned as he wrote it down.

We sat down alongside the other people waiting to get in. In less than two minutes, another Disney associate showed up wearing an earpiece. He looked very official, like Disney CIA.

He came over to us and asked, "Are you the apple-pancakes family?"

I said, "Actually, we go by the 'apple-pancakes gang.'"

He looked at Josh-Brown, extended his hand, and said, "You must be Josh-Brown. My name is Mike. You are famous around here. Please follow me."

We gathered our things and hurried behind our new friend. He escorted us past the entire throng of people. We were somewhat embarrassed by all the attention until we got halfway through the crowd. Then we began enjoying the special treatment. We began to walk a little differently. Our paces slowed. Our facial expressions changed. We were loving the VIP treatment.

We finally made it inside. As the crowd disappeared, there was only one person standing in the lobby: Aunt Bea.

Josh-Brown, who normally doesn't show much emotion or initiate physical contact, walked up to her and fell into her arms. They hugged for what seemed like an hour. As parents, it was powerful to see our son express his emotions. We were crying, taking pictures, and completely absorbed in the moment.

And then my business brain kicked in with a question.

How does Bea do that? How can she create a moment in time that connects with someone on a level that transcends business, special needs, and a decade in time? How does she completely and fully own a moment that inspired people to want to experience her unique brand of magic again?

We didn't just have lunch. We sat and talked to Aunt Bea for a long time, and she told us her own apple-pancakes story.

She said, "Mr. and Mrs. Brown, you probably don't know that when you were here in 2007, I didn't know anything at all about autism. I am passionate about what I do, and I love serving people. From that day until now, I have not stopped learning about the effects of food on children with autism. I cannot thank you enough for what your son has done to make me better."

I was stunned.

She continued. "Another thing you probably don't know is that in 2007 Disney wasn't really equipped to handle special dietary meals for kids like Josh. After your visit, we went to work and created a program to serve kids like Josh, and I am happy to report that in 2016 we will serve over one million kids with special dietary needs. We can't thank you enough for what your son has done for our business."

More stunned-ness.

She continued. "I have shared the apple-pancakes story at employee meetings and with all my teammates. We aspire for the apple-pancakes experience to be the gold standard for how we serve our customers in all of our restaurants."

I was speechless.

Bea taught me a powerful truth that day: Influence is a two-way street. I was completely aware of the positive influence that Bea had on our family. In fact, I have shared the apple-pancakes story in speeches to thousands of people. It has had a profound influence on my life.

I had no idea about the influence that Josh-Brown had on Bea and the Disney organization.

BECOMING A HERO

Are you being held back because of what you perceive someone else thinks? Maybe it is time to release those chains and focus on becoming your very best. You will become what you believe, not what others perceive.

Bea was a hero because she paid attention to a need that no one else expressed. Look around. Are there people surrounding you who could use your attention right now?

You may never know the positive influence that you have on others. Josh-Brown had no idea how he was influencing one of the world's best service organizations to become even greater. You may have that powerful influence as well without being aware of how you helped someone become greater.

We always think that influence is a one-way street, but it is always a two-way street. Who are you influencing? How are you influencing them? Who is influencing you and how? What can you do to elevate the experience others have with you?

chapter 7

Your World Needs a Hero

Regardless of where you live, the stage of life that you are in, or how you feel about being a hero, the world around you needs a hero. The people you see every day need to be influenced by the extraordinary person you were born to be—a talented, gifted, and positive person who brings great things to your world.

Within you lives a hero. It is easy to recognize the heroes around you. Now is the time to discover the hero within you. It's time to develop your unique qualities and use them to make a positive impact in the world and on your life.

What's Your Kryptonite?

Do you remember Superman and the superhuman acts he performed for the good of mankind? Of course you do, but do you remember what robbed Superman of all his power?

It was kryptonite ... the one thing that took away his greatness. It left him powerless and weak, helpless and unable to make any significant contribution to the world. It made him vulnerable, and he became an easy target. Kryptonite was imposed on Superman by external forces intent on destroying him and keeping him from fulfilling his destiny.

For you to be a hero, you have to face and conquer your own kryptonite. What is robbing you of your power? What is stealing your greatness and leaving you helpless, hopeless, or weak? What external force is keeping you from your best life?

If you are like most, the number one source of kryptonite in your life is other people. It may sound harsh, but many people are held back by critics who enjoy tearing you down and telling you everything you are doing wrong. They ride in on their white horses and pretend to be the smartest people in the room. They tell you you're not good enough and that you don't have what it takes.

For some people, their kryptonite is voices from the past reminding them of failures and mistakes. They drag around the worst of yesterday to keep them from moving boldly and powerfully into their future. They paint a vision for tomorrow that looks terrifyingly like their past. They want to hold you back and keep you down in the muck and mire of negative thinking and self-criticism.

What can you do? Do what Superman would do. He would muster every ounce of strength he had to get away from the kryptonite. He would crawl, scratch, and claw his way to safety.

You may be thinking, "Superman is a fictional character. He isn't real, and you are telling me to do what he would do?"

You are right. He isn't real. But then again, most of the things that hold people back aren't real, either. What holds most people back is made up ... pure fiction. The reality is that unless you listen to them, other people's opinions have no bearing on what is in you and what you are capable of.

Whatever the kryptonite is in your life, you must do everything within your power to rise up and move in the other direction. Dig deep. Find the courage and strength to claw, scratch, and crawl away from whatever is holding you back.

The only way things will be different in your life is for you to do things differently. Whatever got you to your current place is not enough to get you to the next level. Regardless of how much success or failure you've experienced thus far, to get to a better place, you must change your thinking, learn new skills, and develop new habits. It is impossible to just stay the same. You are either moving forward or sliding backward.

Worse than Kryptonite

While kryptonite robbed Superman of his power, made him weak, and took away his gifts, there was something else that did the same thing, something more powerful than kryptonite. It was more dangerous, more insidious, and more destructive, because it wasn't inflicted upon him by an outside force. It came from within … it was his choice.

Superman chose to be Clark Kent more often than Superman. He made a decision to be ordinary most of the time. To fit in. To be average. To hide his gifts and abilities. To keep his "super-ness" from a world that so desperately needed it.

What choices are you making that are keeping your superhuman gifts from your world? What decisions are keeping you stuck as an ordinary person? What can you do right now to bring forth your extraordinary self and begin to show up to deliver your best to the people around you? What decisions do you need to make that will begin to move you closer to the life you want?

Pick one action and do something about it right now. Maybe it's a phone call you need to make, a class you need to take, or a mentor you need to reach out to. Maybe you need to tell someone you are sorry and ask for forgiveness. Maybe it's time to let go of the baggage you've been dragging around from your past. It's time to let go of the conversations and voices in your head that say you aren't good enough and that you can't win.

Maybe you need to take inventory of your talents, gifts, and abilities and begin to see yourself as the extraordinary person you are. Perhaps you should start selling yourself on you instead of listening to the voices of your critics.

It is time to stop being ordinary and become everything you were born to be. To embrace the superhuman-being within you and give the world your best self each and every day.

You need to be a hero. Your world needs you to become a hero. It could begin right now, right where you are.

Your Heroes Need Encouragement

When you decide to be a hero, you will need encouragement. In fact, your heroes need encouragement as well. The world is full of discouragers; you can become a hero simply by encouraging others along the way.

During an interview, Oprah Winfrey shared that she had interviewed over thirty-five thousand guests on *The Oprah Winfrey Show*. When asked about a common thread shared by all the people she had interviewed, she said that everyone she had ever interviewed sought validation. It didn't matter whether it was President Bush, Sylvester Stallone, or Beyoncé. When the cameras stopped rolling and the lights were turned off, they all leaned over and said, "Was that okay?"

They wanted to know if they had done well. They wanted to be validated. They wanted a little encouragement that they were okay. It didn't matter whether they were the best or worst in the world at what they did or if they were leaders of the free world. They wanted to know if they had done a good job in Oprah's moment.

Everyone in your life, whether you know them well or you've just met, craves validation and longs to be recognized for their unique gifts. The concept of validation is a powerful revelation. This single idea can change everything in your life, both personally and professionally. The people in your life, at work and at home, are desperately seeking evidence that they matter to you.

No Random Acts of Kindness

I don't believe in random acts of kindness.

Follow me on this. If you believe that kindness should be random, then you are randomly releasing your ability to be a hero. Kindness and serving others should never be random. It should, in fact, garner high priority and great attention. Your interactions with others should be very specific, calculated, and intentional about treating them well.

Randomness means you can ignore your hero responsibility and treat others with kindness when it tickles your fancy to do so, is convenient, or easy.

It's easy to be kind when everything is going your way. When times are tough, you will discover one of the greatest truths in life: It is incredibly difficult to be weighed down by your problems when you are helping other people get out from underneath theirs. Read that again: **It is incredibly difficult to be weighed down by your problems when you are helping other people get out from underneath theirs.**

Your Personal Brand

Are you willing to step up and take a stand? Everyone you are around has already figured out what is non-negotiable for you, even if you haven't.

The people who know you could write down one sentence about what you stand for based on how they see you treat people and how you do what you do. Why don't you take a stab at writing down what they might say? Go ahead. Give it a shot:

_____

_____

Your personal brand is being perpetuated with every encounter, every interaction. And, it grows larger every time you show up. Your reputation is a powerful force. It enters before you and announces your arrival. It lingers long after you leave a room.

Think about what lingers after you push "send," hang up the phone, or leave the room. How do people react when they see your name in their inbox or on their caller ID? Are they eager to accept your call, or do they prefer to "let it go to voicemail"? Their perception of your personal brand determines how they respond to you.

One of the great discoveries I have made while studying thousands of people is that long-term, sustained, high performance is the result of an intense focus and unrelenting pursuit of delivering heroic experiences for the people they serve.

People are drawn to heroes. They return to them again and again, spending their dollars, time, and attention. They give them approval, admiration, and the precious gift of their loyalty. They are fans.

You can be that hero.

BECOMING A HERO

What is your kryptonite? What decisions are keeping you stuck as an ordinary person? What can you do right now to bring forth your extraordinary self and begin to show up to deliver your best to the people around you?

Heroes need validation. Take a moment and think of your heroes. Then, make sure they know that they are your hero and why.

Everyone has a personal brand. How would you describe the brand that others see in you?

What choices do you need to make that will begin to move you closer to becoming the hero you want to be?

chapter 8

My Story

My dad was a Navy man, and he is one of my heroes. When I was born, he was stationed in Long Beach, California. Shortly after I arrived, he left the U.S. Navy and began his new life as a civilian. We moved to Michigan, and dad went to work in a factory where he would become a supervisor. He worked there until he retired.

I grew up in a typical blue-collar home. My parents were loving, and we were happy for the most part. My dad worked while my mom stayed home and took care of three kids. We were poor but didn't realize it because we had everything we needed. In hindsight, I guess we really weren't poor at all. We just didn't have a lot of money.

When I think about heroes, I am reminded of a kid I went to school with. I had literally known him all my life. One day when he was in the tenth grade, he disappeared. He was smart, athletic, and popular. He seemed to have everything going for him, but he just vanished.

Everyone wondered what happened. People talked about him and speculated. Had he moved away? Was he on drugs? Maybe he died. Rumors circulated. After a while, everyone just stopped talking about him. Life went on.

Years later, we learned the rest of his story. He had been betrayed by a trusted adult in his life. A close family friend had let him down in an unimaginable way. Back then you didn't talk about those things, least of all to your parents. It didn't take long before he was broken, tired, and scared.

Late one night he stuffed everything he owned into a big, green duffle bag. The following morning, he left for school and disappeared. He never went home again. He floundered around, made bad choices, and spent time with the wrong people. He was homeless part of the time. When he wasn't homeless, he was wearing out his welcome with people who were kind enough to provide him a place to stay.

His life spun out of control. He contemplated suicide. He was desperate and frustrated and didn't know what to do. His life was littered with one failure after another: divorce, lost jobs, and missed opportunities. With a mixed-up perception of himself, he barely recognized that kid who used to have so much promise.

I know exactly how he felt.

I was that kid.

I was the kid whose picture-perfect life had been shattered. Broken. Desperate. Searching for answers. I was thoroughly convinced my life didn't matter … until a hero showed up.

A Hero Named David

My first mentor was a man named David. He was a gruff, no-nonsense sales guy from South Texas. David helped me pull my life out of the ditch by teaching me about sales and about life.

He taught me how to create a vision for my life that was far different from my past. He would tell me,

"*If your vision is big enough, the odds don't matter!*" In other words, nothing can beat the odds like a giant-sized vision for your life.

David didn't allow me to wallow in self-pity. He would not allow negativity and victim-thinking. He didn't let me hide behind my past and the things that had happened to me. When I would lash out and say, "You don't understand. My life hasn't been fair!" he would glare at me and, in a firm and steady tone, say, "Listen to me, son. Life is completely fair. Nobody gets out unscathed. You think you are the only one with problems? Guess again. The difference between happiness and misery is as simple as choosing which one you want and then doing the work to make it happen. You can't work on your future while you're stuck in the past."

David held me to a higher standard than I held myself. That's what real friends and mentors do. I've heard people say their closest friends accept them as they are. I believe that people who care the most about you will hold you accountable to becoming the best version of yourself. They aren't going to buy your excuses. They won't let you slide by with anything other than the very best version of you.

Why? Because they know what's in you. They know what you've got to offer. Holding people accountable to their talents, gifts, and abilities is what heroes do.

David poured ideas into my young mind that would slowly begin to turn the tide of uncertainty in my life. The waves of desperation began to subside, and a new calm emerged that I had longed for since the night I packed that big, green duffle bag. He helped me get on my feet and take responsibility for my life.

Heroes Need Heroes

One day several years later, David called me. His words were shocking and scary: "Kevin, I've got cancer. Stage 4 lung cancer. Doc says I have six months to live. Says I should get a haircut because it will be my last."

I was shocked. I had a million thoughts racing through my mind but couldn't form a single word. I finally squeezed out the words, "I am so sorry."

In true David fashion, he fired back, "Don't be sorry for me. This just means I need to get to work."

I said, "What are you going to do with six months to live?"

He said, "I am going to move in with my mother-in-law." He paused for a few seconds and continued, "It will be the longest six months of my life."

David's sense of humor and quick wit were infectious. I couldn't help but laugh. I said, "Quit goofing around, man. What are you going to do?"

"I am going to go to work on me, Kevin. This didn't just happen. It's the byproduct of poor choices and bad habits. I got arrogant. Thought I was bulletproof. I got away from the fundamentals of good living. This is on me, and now I need to go 'to work.'"

That was the David I knew so well. A fighter. A believer.

I said, "What can I do?"

He said, "Pray."

So, I did.

Expect a Miracle

I hung up the phone and began to cry. My hero was dying.

I turned to a mutual friend of mine and David's, a motivational teacher named Dwight O'Neil. I told Dwight what I had just heard on the phone and asked him to call David.

Dwight looked at me and said, "Expect a miracle."

So, I did.

Dwight called David and began helping him get his mind right for the battle ahead. He gave him visualization exercises and self-talk strategies to keep his mind strong while he readied himself for war.

David was indeed a warrior. Everything he ever taught me was on full display. He walked his talk. He fought hard. Standing at death's door, he kept fighting. He kept working. He kept believing in his miracle.

And he kept getting his miracle.

Ten years after his six-month diagnosis, we were sitting on David's patio in Texas. He had beaten cancer four times in ten years. He had letters from two doctors confirming that it had, in fact, vanished from his body.

However, shortly after that visit, I received a call from David: "Kevin, my cancer is back for a fifth time, and it is back with a vengeance. I am tired. I'd love to see you before I go."

I was living in Tennessee. I packed a few items and rushed out the door. I made the fourteen-hour trip in twelve. I was anxious to see him.

When I walked into David's house, I saw a man sitting in a recliner. He didn't look like my old friend, but I recognized his voice. David had two daughters who helped him out of his chair. He met me halfway across the living room floor and squeezed me tighter than he ever had. I felt like he was going to break me in two.

I could feel his whiskers against my cheek. They were wet as he started to cry.

He whispered in my ear, "I am glad you're home, son. Now all my kids are here. Let's go outside and sit for a minute." We sat outside and sipped sweet tea and other things. We reminisced. We laughed and cried. Two hours went by in the blink of an eye. And then he was quiet.

David reached over to grab my arm but missed. He ended up grabbing my foot instead. He was a proud man and would never want me to know he wasn't actually aiming for my foot. So, he just held my foot. He started shaking it back and forth, which meant he was nervous. A tear rolled down his cheek.

His voice quivered as he said, "I am proud of you, Kevin." Those were very powerful words. I never outgrew my desire to hear them. He continued. "I love you, and I am going to miss you." He looked at me and said, "I just want to know that it mattered, Kevin."

"That what mattered?" I asked.

"I just want to know that my time on earth mattered—that it counted for something. Will anyone even know I was here?" He kept asking questions. "Did I work hard enough? Did I serve enough? Did I give enough? Did I love enough? Because right now, I'm not so sure. I am about to meet my maker, and I can't get one minute back. I can't change one thing that I did or didn't do."

He took a deep breath and, after a long exhale, he said, "I don't know. I guess it doesn't really matter now."

I reached over and put my hand on his shoulder. "Listen to me," I said softly. "Your life matters, my friend. First of all, you not only changed a life, you *saved* a life. I wouldn't even be here today without you. I owe you everything."

I squeezed his shoulder and leaned toward him. "I love you, David. I am going to miss you for sure. But it's time for you to rest. You did enough. You left a mark that cannot be erased. I am proud of you. You are my best friend. My mentor. My coach. Thank you for being my other dad."

We sat in silence until it was time to say goodbye.

It was the last time I would see him.

I have told my story about David's positive influence on my life to thousands of people whom David will never meet. He has influenced all of them.

I believe that for every person you've touched in a positive way, there are hundreds, perhaps thousands, of other lives that have been influenced. People have been the beneficiaries of your kindness, your encouragement, or your mentoring. I believe that for every life you leave better than you found it, those people pour it into others, multiplying your influence exponentially.

That is what David has done for every person who has heard me share his story.

It's Called "Self-Help" for a Reason

David didn't make the changes for me. He kept me on track and helped me correct my course along the way. The work part was up to me. I had to take what he taught me and apply it. It was up to me to make better decisions and choose a different path. It was up to me to let go of my past and embrace my future.

Many times, I've watched people who are unwilling to do the work. They just want the result. They want a better life and bigger returns. They want a better marriage, successful career, great kids. They want to be happy. But they aren't willing to do what it takes to have those things. The sad truth is it takes more work, energy, and stress *not* to have them—to stay where they are and remain small in a big world.

It's called "self-help" for a reason. I am a self-help junkie. I came to understand that until I changed, nothing would change. Then when I began changing, everything began changing for me. Now is a good time to go to work on yourself to become the best possible version of you.

BECOMING A HERO

A simple change in your thinking can have a profound and lasting influence on your life. What is your big vision? What is it that you would dare to do if success was guaranteed? How would you rewrite the story of your life beginning now? Who must you become to bring your vision into reality?

Look around you. Is there anyone who could use your words of encouragement? Can you be a hero to them right now? No one is beyond hope. Maybe you can be the "David" to provide someone a way out of the ditch that has them stuck.

chapter 9

Unleashing Your Hero

This is the final chapter of *The Hero Effect*. Is this the end of your journey with me? I hope not. My desire is that you are prepared to unleash your hero.

When I was stuck creating my speech about heroes, Lisa convinced me to look at my life and tell my story. She was right. I quickly discovered that there were heroes all around me. I hope that you learned from some of my heroes … Bea, Josh-Brown, both Lisas, and David. More importantly, I hope that you will look in your own mirror, identify your heroes, and make the choice to become an extraordinary hero for those around you.

The speech that began with a blank sheet of yellow paper changed my life. Since that first speech, I have had the privilege of delivering *The Hero Effect* message to thousands of people.

My hero journey was not smooth. Yours probably will not be, either. In fact, you will experience plenty of bumps along the way.

Years ago, Josh, Lisa, and I were on a flight from Nashville to Los Angeles. The flight was a rough, bumpy ride. I travel a lot, and turbulence doesn't get my attention very often, but Lisa and Josh had never experienced that kind of instability in flight.

Josh was about ten years old and seated between Lisa and me when the plane started to bounce. He reached over and took ahold of our hands. Then, he leaned over to me and whispered, "Dad, are there bumpy roads in heaven?"

I love the innocence of his question, the pure and simple thinking of a young boy when the sky above the clouds got bumpy.

I leaned over and whispered back, "No, son. There are no bumpy roads in heaven. It's just a little bumpy getting there, that's all."

Life is a little bumpy. Things don't always go the way we planned, and sometimes unexpected things happen to us. We don't always know when the bumps are going to come or when we will face our toughest moments. That's why our world needs heroes: to smooth out the rough spots and help people get back on the road of life.

Everything Speaks

My friend and branding expert Jeffrey Buntin Jr. helps some of the best business brands tell their stories well. His philosophy and approach to branding is this: Everything speaks. When I asked Jeffrey to give me the core of the "everything speaks" philosophy, here is what he said: "'Everything speaks' is about establishing a code with yourself for how you live. It is about synchronizing your values, behaviors, and communication with others. It's about putting the authentic you at the center of the life experiences you were meant to have. 'Everything speaks' applies to your personal life, relationships, and to your work."

I agree. Everything and everyone's actions send a message. From the person manning the front counter to the person sitting in the corner office, everyone tells their story—good, bad, or otherwise.

Your gestures, words, body language, and tone all communicate to the people around you exactly who you are and what their experience with you is going to be like.

"Everything speaks" is a vitally important concept. Someone is watching all the time. Not only are they watching, they are locked and loaded, ready to record on a moment's notice and then blitz social media with your magic or misfortune.

I am fascinated when I hear people make excuses for how they act. They will usually recuse themselves from the hot seat by proclaiming something along the lines of "that's just the way I am."

Let me make this crystal clear: The way you are is the way you choose to be. It's absolutely your decision to act the way you do. You may have some genetic predisposition or a life of conditioning that influences your behavior. But make no mistake about it, you are who you are and do what you do because you choose to be that way and do those things.

What's amazing is that the people around you will often make excuses for you. They will say things like, "He didn't mean to say that," or "She was just venting. You know she has been through a lot lately," or "He really is a good person underneath."

Really? You are who you are, what you believe, and where you are because of the choices you make. Heroes are clear about the responsibility that comes with the job. They understand that they may not be able to control circumstances, but they can most certainly control how they respond to circumstances, situations, and what other people do.

There's a line from the movie *Batman Begins* that sums it up perfectly: "It's not who you are underneath. It's what you do that defines you." Indeed, everything speaks. What do your actions say about you?

Don't Suck

Not long ago, I was speaking to a prestigious group of successful entrepreneurs and business owners. I was nervous. I always get nervous. I believe that being anxious means you care. I read that comedian George Burns threw up before every performance. I can relate to that.

I was sitting backstage collecting my thoughts and

making some last-minute notes. Through the door walked the CEO. Big, tall, and athletic-looking man. He was wearing an expensive suit and a nice watch. I don't know what kind of cologne he had on, but it smelled like money.

He came over and introduced himself with a handshake. He looked at me and said, "I am really glad you are here, Kevin. This is a great group of successful people. They need to be inspired to keep doing great things. They also need to be reminded of what got them here and what keeps them here. This is an important message, and I appreciate your being here."

I relaxed a little. I knew he was on my side. He understood what I was about and embraced my story. As he got up to leave, he put his hand on my shoulder and gave it a little squeeze. He looked down at me and said, "Don't suck!"

Then I got nervous again. From that day until now, whenever I am blessed to take the stage, I hear his voice and think about those words: Don't suck.

People don't care how many times I have been amazing in the past or the number of standing ovations I have received. They don't care what I promise to do in the future. They do care about whether or not I brought my very best to the platform this time. Can I stand and deliver in that moment? That's what they care about.

I contend that the people in your life are wondering the same thing. When you step onto your platform, people are hoping you don't suck. They are hoping you bring your very best to the present moment. They are hoping that you can stand and deliver on the promises you've made.

Can you? Do you?

Heroes own the moments that matter, and they show up every day better than they were yesterday. They bring the best of themselves to every endeavor and never take for granted the blessed opportunity to serve others. Who is better today because you showed up and didn't suck? Who is moving forward because you took the time to teach, train, guide, and mentor? Who has more in his or her life today because of your kindness?

Heroes are planters. They plant ideas, principles, hope, and encouragement in those around them.

There's an old saying that if you cut an apple, you can count the seeds in the apple. But if you will plant those seeds, you can never count the apples that come from those seeds. What are you planting in the lives of others?

The Legacy of a HERO

After you take your last breath, someone will probably summarize your entire life in a few words and carve it in a piece of stone. What will they say about you? How will you be remembered? Doesn't it make sense to choose, right here and now, what they will write on your rock?

You decide what your legacy will be. You decide what will live on after you are gone. You decide what the story line of your life will be.

The time to unleash the hero within you is now. Now is the time to discover your extraordinary self, show up every day, and choose *not* to be ordinary. Now is the time to **h**elp people—with no strings attached. Don't wait to create an **e**xceptional experience for the people you serve. Begin taking **r**esponsibility for your attitude, actions, and results right now, and see life through the lens of **o**ptimism.

If you do these things, I am absolutely convinced it will change your life. And it will change the world around you. Your world needs the extraordinary person within you to show up every day to lead, love, and serve.

Our world needs your uniqueness to color it with the brilliance that only you possess. We need you to use the talents, gifts, and abilities that are uniquely yours to leave an indelible impression.

My friend, the time to unleash the hero within you is now.

About the Author

Kevin Brown understands what drives organizational excellence and customer loyalty. He knows firsthand how great brands think, feel, and act. He is a branding and culture expert with a career in franchise development that spans thirty years.

Kevin helped build a little-known family business into the No. 1 brand in their industry with revenues reaching $2 billion. Along the way, he has learned how to overcome adversity, deal with change, and create a culture that drives organizational excellence and customer loyalty.

In 2017, Kevin retired from corporate America to take his message around the world. Today, he is recognized as one of the best inspirational speakers in the world. His *The Hero Effect* keynote has been delivered to hundreds of thousands of people worldwide, including as a featured keynote at the 2016 Presidential National Prayer Breakfast business meeting.

Invite Kevin Brown
to your organization
for an inspiring, dynamic
The Hero Effect keynote.

Kevin is a masterful storyteller with a powerful blend of humor, relevant insights, and actionable takeaways that make him a favorite among audience members. His dynamic delivery will bring your event to life!

Here are examples of how Kevin has inspired his audiences:

> "Your presentation was the highlight of our meeting. Your message was personal, heartfelt, and timeless, as it reminded all of us about being everyday heroes."

> "Every once in a while, if you're lucky, you cross paths with greatness. Individuals who make you better by just being in their presence. Kevin Brown is one of those people."

> "Your passion and story really resonated with people here … your closing keynote was like the bottom of the ninth inning with the score tied and you walked up and hit a grand-slam home run for the walkoff win!! Bottom line: Kevin … simply put … you rocked it when you were here!"

"YOU WERE AWESOME! You have a gift. You are a great storyteller and connect with people on such an emotional level. And your humor is great on top of it all. I could not have been more pleased and am blessed to have met you. Thanks for making our event special."

"We had about 500 employees attend his presentation. We laughed, cried, and walked away inspired to be everyday heroes."

Invite Kevin Brown to inspire your team and help create greater success for your organization. Each presentation is designed to set a solid foundation for both organizational and personal success.

Contact info@KevinBrownSpeaks.com.

The Hero Effect Package

Includes all books pictured for
only $129⁹⁵!
(Reg. price $163)

For additional leadership resources,
visit us at www.**CornerStoneLeadership**.com

Thank you for reading *The Hero Effect*!

We hope it has assisted you in your quest
for personal and professional growth.
CornerStone Leadership's mission is to
fuel knowledge with practical resources that will
accelerate your success and life satisfaction!

CornerStone
Leadership Institute
www.**CornerStoneLeadership**.com